DANYELLE M. ADDESSO

All the Things I Never Said

Contents

II   Clarity

III   Healing

Author's Note & Content Warning

The last words he left me claimed I kept everything inside. As if speaking to him, as if *asking* him not to hurt me could have changed everything. His audacious goodbye haunted me. Words became both my curse and my catalyst, daring me to speak. So, this collection is everything I never said. Every argument, lyric, secret, scribble, thought, and ugly truth in my diary turned to poetry from my soul.

This book is not light. It leads you through darkness that nearly shattered me, clarity that opened my eyes, and healing I never thought I would reach. Within these pages are pieces of me, and with them, truths that may weigh heavy in your hands.

This book contains:

- Emotional and narcissistic abuse
- Gaslighting, manipulation, and control
- Depression, anxiety, and panic attacks
- Isolation, loss of identity, and self-worth
- Infidelity and betrayal
- Degradation in intimacy
- Medical neglect and slut-shaming
- Miscarriage and pregnancy loss (with graphic description of blood)
- The cycle of love-bombing, devaluation, discard, and hoovering

If these subjects are difficult for you, please take care. Step away when you need to. Breathe. Come back only if it feels right.

I dedicate this to anyone who might recognize themselves in these words. To anyone who has lived through the cruelty of narcissistic abuse. To anyone who has ever been told avoiding abuse, was as simple as asking not to be broken.

Thank you for holding these pages with me.

I

Darkness

Fragments of Me

This story is fractured.
  Bits of a soul scattered,
  like glass across the floor.
  I pick up what I can,
  but some pieces are gone forever.
  These pages,
  my evidence, my letters, my confessions,
  a retelling of events,
  ugly, broken, loved, damaged, beautiful.
  They were once to prove I wasn't crazy,
  and now
  these words are for you.
  For anyone questioning their reality,
  lost in confusion,
  doubting themselves,
  unable to recall who they were
  before the lies.
  This is my chaos,
  my truth,
  my voice,
  everything I never said.

The End

The end is often the best place to begin.

Silence

No one tells you how loud silence is,
    the first time you step into a home emptied of them.
    True silence,
    creates a pitch so sharp it splits the air.
    You clear your throat,
    play music,
    rub your praying hands until they burn,
    but nothing kills it.
    My thoughts break silence,
    pounding a drumbeat in my chest.
    Alone.
    Again.
    Always.
    Other thoughts follow like stones through stained glass.
    Broken, damaged, mistake.
    Nine years of swallowing lies for supper,
    and still I said amen.
    Still I water the graveyard grass.
    Maybe I left the monster.
    Maybe I left the only love I'll ever know.
    The price of peace was silence,
    and it devours.

Phantom Weight

His ghost walks the walls of this house.
  I am cold.
  Through the plaster,
  he drifts.
  He moans.
  Phantom weight pressing down,
  an invisible body sinking into the sheets beside me.
  Arms of smoke hold me,
  his ghostly voice breathes in my ear,
  "you will never be free of me."

The House Screamed

Every surface shouted his name.
　The counter
　still warm from his hands,
　a touch that turned to chains.
　The bathroom floor
　where I folded into myself,
　while his rage shook the walls.
　The guest room,
　his kingdom,
　no guest ever welcome.
　The stairs echoed his descent,
　phantom footsteps coming for me.
　The front door still braced,
　like it expected his key.
　Every room shouted.
　Every wall bled.
　Every object screamed his name.
　The house was not shelter,
　the house was him.
　And I collapsed inside it,
　crushed by the weight of his absence,
　crushed by the screaming walls
　I could not silence.

Downpour

Sometimes I relive the final car ride,
   the final downpour that ended it all.
   Rain hammering the windshield.
   Relentless.
   A holiday trip to see family,
   supposed to be normal, happy.
   Turned into a nightmare.
   He yelled. Scolded. Insulted.
   Every word a strike,
   sharper than the last.
   Terror coiled in my stomach.
   Is this my life?
   This fear.
   This storm I cannot escape?
   Terrible thoughts.
   He had never raised a hand to me.
   But tonight,
   tonight I wondered,
   if he could.
   If he might tilt the wheel
   just a little to the left,
   drive us into a ditch
   or another car
   and end it all.

I had never felt fear like this.
Questioning the man I had spent years loving.
Hateful words boomed like thunder.
"I'm just trying to wrap my head around this whole trip"
"Your family doesn't love you"
"I should just find the nearest airport and fly home"
"You're so selfish"
again and again.
I gripped the seat.
I knew I just had to make it to the destination.
I plotted my escape.
Darkness outside mirrored the darkness inside that car.
For the first time,
I saw it clearly.
I had to get out. Get out of this car. Out of this relationship.
No more excuses.
No more hoping.
No more pretending.
Outside, the storm raged on.
Inside me,
a different storm began.

Tiptoes

Rain streaked the car windows like claw marks.
  He was still screaming
  as we pulled into the driveway.
  On the porch, my family waved.
  Door opens,
  and in the blink of an eye his rage evaporated.
  A smile cracked across his face,
  unnatural, painted on.
  He wrapped them in arms
  that only minutes before were daggers aimed at me.
  For once, I didn't feel crazy.
  For once, I saw it was *him* who was insane.
  Behind the closed guest room door,
  he flung the perfect mask across the room.
  His voice became a storm again,
  snapping, tearing,
  a monster hiding behind human skin.
  I fled to the bathroom mirror.
  My reflection stared back, pale, trembling,
  as if the glass might shatter
  from the weight of what I carried.
  I begged myself to move.
  Pleaded with myself to speak.
  On tiptoes,

I crept down the hall
afraid to make a sound.
I reached my parent's door.
They looked at me with confusion,
and I collapsed.
The words burst out,
raw, feral, unstoppable.
"I need help."
That night, he left.
But his shadow stayed behind.
No longer his,
now mine to name,
and mine to cast out.

Evidence

The night I left him,
   I still loved him.
   That was the hardest part.
   Love blurred the edges and softened the blows,
   made me question if any of it was real.
   Was I making it up?
   My mind betrayed me,
   convincing me to go back.
   So I wrote a list,
   line after line,
   detailing every cruel word he spat at me.
   Dates like gravestones.
   Each one a wound I couldn't deny.
   Each one proof I wasn't imagining it.
   Evidence.
   A record.
   Because without the record,
   I might forget.
   And if I forget,
   I might forgive.
   And if I forgive,
   I might return.
   And if I return,
   I will not survive.

Between Seasons

He was warmth, then winter.
  One moment sunlight,
  kisses on my cheek.
  The next, a raging storm
  never in the forecast.
  Every smile had an edge,
  every compliment, a catch.
  Hot, then cold,
  and I was left guessing
  which version of him
  I'd have to survive today.
  I learned to live on shifting ground,
  erasing parts of myself
  to soften his moods.
  If I did the thing,
  it was wrong.
  If I didn't,
  it was worse.
  He was winter and summer,
  and I was stuck
  between seasons.

Monster in the Mirror

In public,
    he is a golden god.
    Every smile sparkles,
    every word velvet.
    Crowds bend toward him
    like sunflowers to light.
    Who would ever believe me?
    I don't believe me.
    If he shines this bright,
    then I must be the rot.
    The worst girlfriend alive.
    But when the door closes
    at the end of the night,
    he hangs the mask on the rack.
    Somehow the night was ruined.
    My fault.
    He says my friends are pathetic.
    He says his friends are fake.
    He wishes I looked like her.
    He wishes I was anyone but me.
    I swallow the bile
    of his truth whole.
    Tell myself I imagined it.
    Tell myself I'll do better.

But in the mirror stares the monster,
not him,
but me.

The Mask

He built it from me.
   Every secret I confessed,
   every dream I bared
   stitched into his disguise.
   A mask of mirrors reflecting
   my laugh, my faith,
   my wants, my words.
   Too good to be true or
   just good enough to bind me?
   Slip.
   A flash of a stranger's cruel eyes.
   I flinch.
   He smiles.
   The mask snaps back on.
   You imagined it.
   And I believed.
   Again.
   Again.
   Again.
   I looked at the mask
   not the face beneath.
   Hypnotized.
   Because he made me believe
   the face staring back

was the other half of my soul.

Needle Love

He was my drug.
   When he was gone
   my skin itched,
   my body shook,
   my thoughts clawed at the walls.
   Withdrawal felt like dying.
   I knew he was poison,
   sweet relief wrapped in venom.
   He injected himself into me,
   and I begged for it,
   even as it burned my veins.
   The second the high hit
   clarity would crash down.
   I'd see him,
   the yelling
   the names
   the madness.
   I tried to suck the venom back out,
   spit him from my bloodstream,
   scrape him off my skin.
   I told myself,
   He's poison! Stop it!
   He's poison. Stop it.
   He's poison… Stop it…

But even as I chanted,
I rolled up my sleeve,
tapped my vein,
waiting for the next hit
I already hated.

Addict

I didn't cut him out.
  I left a crack,
  just enough space
  for him to slip inside.
  Daily doses
  of attention,
  sweet words that tasted like relief,
  but were poison in disguise.
I told myself I was in control.
I had the power now.
I could turn him off anytime.
We talked all day,
and I swallowed his love
like a heroin addict
looking for a fix,
chasing a high
I already knew would kill me.
He fed me carefully,
needle in my vein,
IV dripped slowly,
poison disguised as care.
I lied to myself that I was strong,
that I could hold the line.
But each message, each call,

tightened his grip.
And I craved it.
And I drank it.
And I suffered.

Safe Vines

Each time I reached for the world outside,
   he sighed as if I left him
   to starve in an empty room.
   "You won't have fun,"
   he taunted,
   "your sister doesn't like you.
   Your family doesn't care.
   They left you."
   I carried his words,
   vines woven around my flesh.
   His echo curled tighter,
   thorns in the vine around my ribs.
   "Your friends hate you,
   they only pity you.
   I'm the only one who understands you."
   And when I returned,
   the house, a cathedral of silence.
   The loneliest I've ever been
   sitting in the same house
   while he pretended
   I wasn't there.
   The ugly truth is
   it's easier to wither inside these ivy walls.
   It's safer not to go outside at all.

Who Would Love You?

"Go ahead and leave me. Who could ever love you besides me?"
His question dressed as mercy,
a noose braided into a compliment.
I left anyway.
He offered nothing I ever needed.

Cut from the Frame

He curates his life
  like a highlight reel,
  all golden hours and staged smiles.
  But the camera stops
  just before it reaches me.
  In his curated world,
  he lives like he is single.
  Maybe he is.
  Because where am I?
  Nowhere.
  I am a ghost at the edge of his lens.
  I try to show him.
  I write love into captions.
  Hold him up so the world can see.
  See how proud I am that he is mine.
  I show him how I wish to be treated.
  He never learns.
  And then,
  I stop.
  My feed empties,
  my life dissolves,
  my friends drift away.
  The silence swallows me whole.
  Maybe I am hideous.

Maybe I am unworthy of the frame.
My body not seventeen anymore,
my face tired,
my existence an embarrassment.
He hates me.
So I learn to hate me, too.

The Prison I Knew

A chair beneath the door tonight.
   One lock isn't enough.
   Two locks aren't enough.
   Press wood against wood,
   my only fortress,
   my only army
   against an enemy I mistook for a friend.

"I was doing you a favor," he said.
   "Pretend I was never here."
   But shadows keep receipts.
   The walls whisper.
   Every sound in the dark
   drags him back into the room.

Progress now a cruel joke.
   One night, one touch,
   and the scaffolding I was building collapses.
   I run back, bloodied,
   to the monster I know.
   His cage is predictable.
   His chains, familiar.
   And what is safety,
   if not choosing the prison where the lock fits best?

Stain

I am stained.
   Flashbacks crawl beneath my skin,
   a plague I cannot wash away.
   His lips dragged across my face,
   a sickening smear I still taste.
   His breath clings to my neck like rot,
   his embrace a snare tightening.
   My mind whispers,
   "endure, it will be over soon."
   My home is a crime scene.
   Every room carries his stain.
   The walls reek of him,
   air hums with his trespass.
   I curse the silence I swallowed,
   the scream I buried.
   Politeness was my coffin, his hands the nails.
   I thank God he didn't press further,
   but gratitude is ash on my tongue.
   Even with the locks turned,
   the chair braced against the door,
   his shadow waits.
   And if I burned this house to ash,
   he would crawl out of the smoke.

You're Okay

I rock myself.
  Back.
  Forth.
  Arms wrapped tight.
  Hands rubbing my own skin.
  Friction.
  Heat.
  Holding myself together.
  you're okay
  you're okay
  you're okay
  Half prayer.
  Half lie.
  But I keep saying it.
  Rocking.
  Rocking.
  Until the chant is louder than my heartbeat.
  You're okay.
  I whisper it to the girl inside me
  curled up and shaking,
  because she needs to hear it.
  Even if I can't.

Overkill

As if on cue,
   he performs love to perfection.
   Every gesture,
   every kiss,
   every thoughtful gift,
   perfectly timed, perfectly placed.
   Kissing my forehead,
   my neck, my cheek, the top of my head.
   Gazing when he thinks I'm not looking,
   singing beautiful chords.
   Bombing me with love.
   Yet I feel doubt.
   I feel mistrust.
   Like it's all a facade.
   I catch myself thinking,
   Overkill.
   He expresses love every single day,
   and I…
   I couldn't.
   He's perfect.
   Was he ever so bad?
   Have I made a grave mistake?

Thorn Game

I pluck a thorn.
  I love him.
  Another.
  I love him not.
  Each prick draws blood,
  my fingers trembling,
  red droplets marking my path
  until it's slick beneath me.
  I slip.
  Fall into his words.
  His voice becomes my truth.
  I stand.
  For a heartbeat, I see.
  He's a lie.
  I'm bleeding.
  Another thorn.
  Another drop.
  I love him.
  I love him not.
  Reality bends.
  He tells me our problems are in my head.
  I start to believe him.
  I can't tell
  if it's my head

or his hands pulling me under.
The stem grows shorter.
The thorns sharper.
I'm playing a game I can't win,
shredding myself
to know the answer.

Mother Figure

I love him,
   but I do not like him.
   Life plays out
   in flickering black and white frames,
   an old film where he cast me
   as the mother figure.
   Caretaker on cue,
   apron tied,
   smile rehearsed.
   I cooked, I cleaned,
   packed his lunch
   and held his hand.
   But he bruised me
   with his tantrums,
   a boy demanding
   a mother I was never meant to play.
   I am not your Donna Reed,
   yet day after day
   this stale film flickers on.

Kissing Villains

His story continues,
   written now in another woman's margins.
   Just like that.
   While he *swore* he loved me.
   While he *begged* me to believe.
   While he *promised* he'd changed.
   He was courting her.
   He was courting me.
   Two scripts, one liar.
   Nine years of my blood,
   my heart scraped raw
   while he rehearsed his new lines
   in someone else's arms.
   There was no warning.
   No slip, no crack, no clue.
   Just like that,
   the mask ripped off,
   and underneath,
   revealed the villain I'd been kissing
   all along.

Discard

He fed me crumbs.
  Little promises,
  soft words,
  empty gestures.
  Look how I've changed.
  Look how I love you.
  Look how I'm better now.
  And I swallowed them
  because numbness
  was easier than the pain of moving on.
  I told myself,
  if he loves me enough, he'll stop hurting me.
  If I wait long enough, he'll become someone else.
  But in one split second the illusion shattered.
  His "love" had already moved.
  A new supply.
  Her.
  And me?
  I was the past.
  No explanation.
  No closure.
  No care.
  Just the discard.
  Nine years reduced

to trash on the curb,
a toy stripped of shine,
kicked into the dark.
The crumbs in my hands spoiled.
The truth cut deeper than his rage ever did.
I wasn't left.
I was discarded.
Abandoned mid sentence.
Erased while breathing.
Replaced before I knew.
And the silence after,
was the cruelest cut of all.

Who Am I to Be Mad?

I was the one who ended it.
  I walked away.
  So who am I to be mad
  that he moved on?
  That's the question
  I circle in my head,
  like punishment.
  But endings weren't endings with him.
  He found me.
  Pulled me back.
  Fed me promises.
  Fed me hope.
  We're not over, he whispered.
  I've changed, he swore.
  I love you, he vowed.
  And I believed,
  because he made belief easier
  than the alternative.
  So I stayed attached,
  threaded to a man
  who had already picked up another spool.
  I broke up with him, yes.
  But he broke me again and again,
  long before and long after the goodbye.

Manipulation doesn't end
when the door shuts.
Abuse doesn't die
because you said the words "it's over."
He made sure of that.
Kept me strung, kept me waiting, kept me his,
until he didn't need me anymore.
So tell me,
who am I to be mad?
The discarded always ask that.
The truth is simple,
I have every right.

Sins in the Shed

Betrayal is buried behind the shed,
   finished or not,
   sin stains the soil.
   You swung the same shovel
   to slit my throat that you used to dig my grave,
   iron biting earth,
   wood slick with your sweat.

You revved the engine of my hearse,
   preening like a victor as I was lowered into silence.
   Mourners drifted past, blind.
   I tried to scream,
   but dirt filled my lungs.
   No bell at my wrist,
   no toll to summon the town to your crime.

Six feet down I accepted the roses you left,
   petals already rotting,
   stems crowned with thorns.
   The dirt hardened in my throat,
   cement sealing secrets with the worms.
   But graves keep records.

And one day,

the roots will claw through your floorboards,
the worms will crawl into your bed,
and my silence will gnaw you from the inside out.

The dead only stay silent...
   until they don't.

Forgotten Keepsakes

Is my picture still tucked in your wallet,
   or was that the first thing to go?
   When I look back at photos,
   I don't see love,
   only painted smiles
   and poisoned memories.
   I buried yours in a box,
   but I daresay what we call keepsakes,
   are just evidence,
   of crimes I kept forgiving.

To Her

I see you with him.
  Your smile looks weathered,
  like you're looking up into a similar mask
  he once wore for me.
  I won't call you a fool.
  I know how easy it is to fall,
  when someone reflects back
  every dream you whispered.
  When he tells you
  you're the one who will save him.
  Did he tell you the same stories?
  The childhood scars?
  The promises of forever?
  The golden future that dulls so quickly to brass?
  It hooked me, too.
  I gave him everything,
  until I was nothing.
  Bones hollowed out,
  ashamed for asking why.
  And part of me is jealous
  that you have the words
  I once believed in.
  He'll drape you in the illusion of safety
  I thought was mine, once, too.

But mostly, I worry.
Because I know the cycle.
I know the mask.
I know the cost.
I hope the ghosts that haunt me
do not follow you.
I hope the lies don't carve you down.
I hope, against what I know,
that your ending
isn't mine.

Exes and Ohs

Oh.
  He's particular, isn't he?

Oh.
  Has he told you the tragic story of his childhood?
  How broken he is?
  How only you can heal him?
  It hooked me, too.
  I thought I was saving him.
  I was only drowning.

Oh.
  Does he tell you you're perfect?
  That you're the only one who understands?
  Careful.
  One day, that "only" becomes "not enough."

Oh.
  Hang on the wrong hook,
  and you'll unleash the beast.
  He never has to say a word,
  we understand the unspoken rules,
  don't we?

Oh.

Have you noticed how quickly his voice can change?
Soft one moment,
sharp the next?
You'll wonder if you imagined it.
I did.

Oh.

Has he called you dramatic yet?
Not yet?
He will.
And you'll start to believe it.
These aren't warnings you'll heed.
I wouldn't have, either.
I only offer them so when he slips,
you'll know
you will not be the first
to bleed from his chaos.

Sadist

He told me once
   he liked to make me mad on purpose.
   Said I was *cute,*
   when my fury flared.
   Wore my hurt like costume jewelry.
   Stringing me up,
   for his sadistic puppet show,
   directing the stage with me as the lead.
   He got off on my hurt,
   drinking my pain like sweet wine
   from a chalice of my bone.
   Toasting to my ruin,
   celebrating the show he wrote from my suffering.

Mania

I hate him.
  I hate him.
  I hate him.
  Did I make this up?
  Did I imagine the names,
  the yelling,
  the gaslight flickering like bad neon?
  No.
  I remember.
  Don't I?
  I remember the walls shaking,
  doors slamming,
  engine roaring,
  tears falling down my cheeks.
  I remember.
  But then I miss him.
  God, I miss him.
  His smell,
  his touch at 2 a.m.,
  the illusion of safety I wore like a second skin.
  Was it even abuse, or am I just broken?
  Was it love, or am I just delusional?
  I circle these questions like a vulture,
  like a clock with no numbers,

spinning, spinning, spinning.
One moment I want to burn it all,
the next I want him back.
He's poison.
He's salvation.
He's a nightmare.
He's the only one who knew me.
I hate him.
I miss him.
I hate myself for missing him.
The room tilts, the world hums,
my own mind
a fun house mirror,
I can't step out of.

No One Is Mad

I didn't think about you this morning.
  I am now.
  So many years of reaching for my phone,
  checking, apologizing, preparing.
  Muscle memory.
  The text before you're angry,
  the call before you accuse.
  Even now my hand twitches,
  "oh no"
  I forgot to text him, he'll be mad.
  But guess what.
  No one is mad.
  No one is waiting to punish me.
  No one is counting my mistakes.
  I am free but my body hasn't learned yet.
  It still ducks,
  still braces,
  still kneels.
  But slowly I am standing up.
  Breaking the reflex.
  Untraining the fear.
  No one is mad at me.
  No one at all.

Cradle of Blood

I recall the pain bent me in half.
  Cramping, tearing,
  blood spilling down my legs,
  The floor stained.
  I drove through it,
  sat in the waiting room
  bleeding into fabric.
  Feet in stirrups,
  eyes fixed on ceiling tiles.
  Doctor's voice,
  cold, condemning.
  Not listening.
  Not seeing.
  Judgment dressed as medicine.
  A verdict, not a diagnosis.
  He branded the letter "A" on my blood soaked clothes.
  I left with nothing but shame.
  Now I ache to know.
  Did I lose a life I didn't know I carried?
  Or was it just blood and nothing more?
  The guilt circles me,
  a ghost I cannot bury.
  No grave.
  No marker.

No proof it was ever real or just haunting hysterics.
Only the memory of blood.
And in the dark,
I hear creaking.
A cradle rocking somewhere,
with no one inside.

Ghost on the Stand

My mind is a courtroom.
   Memories sit in the gallery,
   summoned as witnesses.

A ghost takes the stand
   wearing my face.
   I open my mouth to testify,
   but my voice is struck from the record.

Trauma destroyed the evidence,
   redacting the pages.
   Objection.
   Sustained.

I am left with fragments,
   a case without testimony,
   a life that happened
   but will not stand trial.

I am the Defendant.
   I am the Witness.
   I am the Victim.

The jury stares,

waiting for words I cannot give.
And silence is my sentence.

Labyrinth

Do you think of me the way I think of you?
  Haunted by small, ordinary things?
  A building.
  A stretch of road.
  The salt thick air.
  When you're in Delaware,
  do you see me?
  Do you feel the ghost of broken spring,
  the fight, the tears,
  the weight of what you blamed me for?
  The ocean betrays me.
  You are a siren, pulling me deeper into the depths.
  Every memory splinters like glass,
  a glimmer,
  a shard.
  I can't hold one without bleeding from another.
  So I wander the labyrinth of thought,
  torches burning out,
  walls shifting,
  turning corner after corner.
  Somewhere inside lurks the beast.
  Do you think of me the way I think of you?
  Or am I only a phantom,
  forever hunted,

forever circling this endless maze?

Still Here

I don't miss you anymore.
　　But you're still here.
　　The voice in my head is gone,
　　the one that used to sound like me.
　　Now it sounds like you.
　　When I think, it's you who answers.
　　When I look in the mirror, it's you who critiques.
　　When I watch a movie, your commentary runs beneath the sound,
　　a ghost track I can't switch off.
　　I am living without you.
　　I am healing without you.
　　But somehow you've taken the space in my mind
　　where my own voice should be.
　　You are not here,
　　yet somehow,
　　you are still here.

Broken Shells

I walked the beach,
   footsteps my only company.
   A couple passed, hand in hand.
   He bent, picked up a shell,
   placed it in her palm without ever letting go.
   She smiled, kissed his cheek.
   I thought, *"that is love."*
   Your poltergeist crawled from the shoreline,
   to remind me our love was never deep as the sea.
   You let me walk on broken shells
   that cut my feet,
   blood mixing with the waves,
   and let me call it love.

Glue Trap

They call it inhumane.
  A glue trap.
  Silent, waiting.
  The cruelest death
  stuck, scared,
  nothing to do but wait.
  You were my glue trap.
  Sticky, sweet.
  I stayed too long
  until escape meant
  tearing myself apart.
  I ripped away,
  not a peel
  but a wax strip rip.
  Now I'm free,
  but pieces of me
  still stick to you.
  I walk away
  with phantom limbs,
  missing what I lost,
  even as I breathe again.

The Call

I went to the drugstore,
    just a mundane errand refilling a prescription,
    living my ordinary life
    when the call came.
    Your mom.
    My heart skipped, my words froze,
    I let her speak while I held my breath.
    She wanted to know how I am,
    said she understood why I acted the way I did at the end,
    held no grudge.
    She asked if I was seeing anyone.
    No.
    She asked if I was still in love with you.
    I said I'll always love him,
    but I won't go back.
    She spoke of rebounds,
    unfinished stories,
    how you cry to her saying you still love me,
    that she hopes somehow we might find each other again.
    I told her the truth.
    I am thriving without you.
    She updated me on her life, and yours,
    moves, plans, houses sold,
    her version of peace.

THE CALL

She said you and your new girl will never be us.
On that, I agreed.
I hoped. I prayed, for *her* sake, that they would never be us.
The call ends, but my thoughts continue.
Somewhere deep in the quiet corners of me
a dark, strange part thrives,
knowing you still love me.

Trauma in Fragments

Is healing
    just moving day by day
    with a little less crippling pain?
    Last night I lay in bed
    thinking I'm healed,
    but not.
    The trauma lingers
    like a shadow I no longer stumble over.
    His name no longer breaks me.
    I don't yearn.
    I remember the easy,
    the knowing glances, the inside jokes,
    but the words we shared
    were hollow, just a mockery, nothing of substance.
    I look back at photos, at texts,
    and feel only a faint sadness for a life I used to live
    not mine anymore.

Ghost on the Lawn

A photo resurfaced of us smiling,
   looking into the camera,
   but I remember the truth.
   You were mad that night,
   silent rage hiding behind a pretend smile.
   I was anxious,
   shrinking in my own skin,
   horror caught on film.
   Now I stand where we stood in that photograph,
   and feel your spirit pacing the grass,
   still making me uneasy.
   Cross over.
   Leave me.
   I don't want you here,
   your silence,
   or your haunt.

Empty Apartment

Grief lingers inside these walls.
Boxes line the floor,
small coffins of what once was ours.
It is strange to stand here
on the edge of a life he touched,
knowing I step into rooms
he will never enter,
streets he will never walk,
a future he cannot follow.
I sit inside the empty closet,
the only corner untouched by him.
I wanted to feel
what untouched felt like.
It isn't madness.
It's holy.
But this empty apartment,
will never truly be bare.
These walls will forever carry the weight
of our horror story.

Bouquet of Bees

A bouquet of blooms
  found its way to me today,
  asking for a moment of my time.
  Her words were careful,
  but I heard the doubt beneath them.
  She was starting to see.
  She asked about him, about us.
  And I told her.
  Not everything, not the worst.
  Those were stings for me to bear.
  I wanted to warn the flowers
  before they wilted.
  To tell them his honey
  was only sugar on the tongue.
  Beneath the sweetness
  waited a swarm of bees
  drawn to the jasmine scent
  but eager to sting
  to swarm
  to devour.
  Now the flower knows.
  But will she stay?
  Because once the stems crack,
  no ribbon can hold them.

And already,
the bees are swarming.

Villain

She told me what he said.
How he spoke of me,
degrading and mocking,
turning private truths into public weapons.
Details no one should carry but us
were handed to her like proof.
His stories painting me in shadows,
his words cutting me in absence.
It hurt.
Not because it was true, but because it was ours.
Because even what was broken deserved silence,
deserved privacy.
But that was never his way.
He needed a villain.
And so he painted me one.

I Can't Be Your Savior

I felt explainable sadness
   the day I learned
   she went back.
   But I know what it is to be trapped.
   That stunning disguise of his.
   Floods of love drowning you so sweetly.
   Grenades of lovely words,
   subtlety stinging you.
   Back to start.
   I feel claustrophobic for her.
   I remember her place, but I remember mine, too.
   It is not up to me to save her.
   I can't be a white knight.
   As much as I wish I could.

The Family Stone

I'm watching *The Family Stone.*
   As a child I dreamed of Christmas like this one.
   Family, love, someone to bring home.
   I never had that.
   Year after year,
   I was never happy.
   I remember our first Christmas.
   Seventeen, excited,
   I built him a box brimming with sweetness,
   his favorite candies,
   his favorite snacks,
   every detail chosen with care.

What do I remember now?
   The label he branded into me.
   How I forgot I was only seventeen.
   How I forgot innocence is its own kind of gift.
   How I forgot sweetness
   should have been enough.

Now I see it clearly.
   That was the first stone,
   in a long road of manipulation.
   I hate him.

I hate what he has done to my mind.
I hate how he ruined every holiday.
Sucked the joy out of every special occasion.

The movie flickers on,
a family framed in golden light.
And still I dream,
that maybe one day
I'll finally find it.

If You Ever Hit Play

I used to send you songs,
    hoping the lyrics would tell you everything I couldn't.
    But you never listened,
    and now the playlist has changed.
    Every track how I felt,
    every chorus holds a curse meant for you.
    If you ever hit play, baby,
    you'll finally hear me.
    All the things I never said.
    The soundtrack to your ruin.

The Playlist:
    A Lot More Free — Max McNown
    Better Man — Taylor Swift
    Coma — Taylor Acorn
    Devil Doesn't Bargain — Alec Benjamin
    Happier Than Ever — Billie Eilish
    Hate Me If You Have To — Ella Langley
    Lose You To Love Me — Selena Gomez
    So Long, London — Taylor Swift
    Tolerate It — Taylor Swift
    The Truth — Megan Woods
    Where You Belong — Matt Hansen
    You Should Be Sad — Halsey

You're Losing Me — Taylor Swift

Eggshells

Every Sunday.
  His sandwich.
  Egg.
  Pork roll.
  Bagel, lightly toasted,
  don't burn it.
  A little ketchup,
  not too much.
  Cheese, American or cheddar.
  If the egg breaks,
  ruined.
  If the toast is wrong,
  ruined.
  One slip,
  ruined.
  I cracked eggs
  with trembling hands,
  walking on shells
  before they even hit the pan.
  One sandwich.
  Every Sunday.
  His ritual.
  My test.
  And if I failed,

the eggs would only be the first
to shatter.

II

Clarity

The Look on Her Face

I thought I was telling a story.
  Just an ordinary day in my life,
  the yelling,
  the unspoken rules,
  the ways I tried to keep the peace.
  I expected sympathy,
  maybe laughter,
  the kind you share when love is hard.
  As it tends to be, right?
  But she went still.
  Her eyes widened,
  her mouth half open,
  and horror spread across her face
  like she had just witnessed a car crash
  and I was the one still bleeding.
  That silence,
  that look was the first mirror
  ever held up to my life.
  I heard myself differently then.
  Each detail I spilled
  sounded sharper,
  darker,
  not quirky,
  not normal,

not love.
That was the day I typed words into a search bar
gaslighting,
control,
verbal abuse.
Each word fit like a puzzle piece,
clicking into place,
building an image
I could no longer unsee.
And for the first time,
I named it.
Not weakness.
Not overreaction.
Abuse.

Rewiring

You rarely gave orders.
  No commands,
  no rules taped to the walls.
  But your silences spoke.
  Your sighs.
  The sharp edge of disappointment
  when I did the wrong thing.
  The rare flash of approval
  when I bent myself smaller.
  Little by little
  I learned what pleased you,
  what kept the peace.
  I trained myself to anticipate,
  to shrink,
  to apologize before I'd even sinned.
  You didn't need chains.
  A system of looks and tones,
  that rewired my body
  to obey.
  By the time I noticed,
  I was fluent in a language of survival
  I never meant to learn.

Unrecognizable

I watched him rage
    through his childhood home.
    Spit flying at his mother's face,
    names sharp as glass.
    He threw things.
    He flipped the couch clear across the room.
    The walls shook with his slamming,
    his screaming,
    his endless yelling.
    And I sat there,
    frozen.
    Because if I left,
    he would turn that fury on me.
    So I stayed,
    terrified,
    waiting for the moment
    I'd be next.
    I remember saying,
    "you better never treat me that way"
    as if it were somehow acceptable
    for him to treat her that way.
    As if violence could ever be contained
    to one target.
    That was the sickness of it.

How my reality bent and warped
until it felt almost reasonable
to sit through someone else's torture,
believing it was the price
of keeping myself safe.
But nothing about it was safe.
Nothing about it was love.
It was terror.
And my reality
became unrecognizable.

Reactive

In the midst of one of our fights,
   I tried to swallow the storm,
   to keep the house quiet,
   but his words kept coming
   relentlessly closing in.
   Something snapped.
   Venom leapt from my mouth
   I didn't know I carried.

And that's when he smiled,
   pulled out his phone.
   Hit record.
   "Go ahead," he coaxed.
   "Talk like that now."

My breaking,
   captured as evidence.
   Not of his cruelty,
   but of *mine.*

Later, in the mirror I searched for myself,
   and almost believed
   I was the monster he wanted me to be.

But driving someone to shatter,
   then filming the wreckage,
   does not make you innocent.
   It only proves
   how intentionally you broke them.

Deadly Threats

"Then I should just die,"
   you said,
   holding the threat
   like a blade to my throat.
   I stayed,
   thinking I was saving you.
   But I wasn't your lifeline.
   I was your hostage.
   And every threat
   was another way
   you kept me caged.

Name It

I am *not* crazy.
  Not dramatic.
  Not too sensitive.
  What I was living through,
  it has a name.
  The second-guessing,
  the blank spaces in memory,
  the constant defense,
  the doubt, the exhaustion,
  all of it.
  I searched once,
  and tumbled down the rabbit hole.
  My mind became a detective's board,
  red threads pulling tight
  through years of evidence
  I had buried as excuses.
  Don't sugarcoat it.
  Don't dress it softer.
  Don't protect him.
  Say the ugly word.
  Abuse.

The Body Keeps Score

My body told the truth
  long before I did.
  I was sick.
  Mind in fog, memories slipping like sand.
  My womb refused,
  rejecting poison,
  refusing to risk a life in the soil where I was buried.
  You made me sick.
  But the moment I walked away,
  I started to heal.
  My body kept score.
  You were the disease,
  leaving you was the cure.

Trumpets

When I broke the news of our end,
    no one wept for you.
    Not a single *"I'm sorry to hear it"*,
    not a single person asked why.
    Instead, a chorus rose singing
    "finally."
    As if they had all been waiting,
    quietly,
    for me to leave you behind.
    Old friends, close friends,
    even some of yours,
    admitted what I had not.
    You never deserved me.
    And in their relief,
    I understood.
    Your absence was no tragedy.
    It was freedom,
    a freedom the world celebrated
    long before I picked up the trumpet
    and joined them.

Gaslight Gospel

You preached love,
   then called me crazy.
   A gospel of contradictions,
   written in the same sermon.

Your verses were never holy,
   they were heresy.
   I was devoted to you,
   but you were a false God,
   a cult I never meant to join.

I'll pray for you,
   I wish you no harm,
   but even heaven turns its face
   from false prophets.

The Climb

I wonder if God makes things so unbearable
    we have no choice
    but to change course.
    I lingered in limbo,
    neither staying nor going.
    I prayed for signs,
    but would not see them.
    It took rock bottom
    to strip my vision clean.
    And there it was,
    the ladder He had built for me.
    So I started to climb.

Resuscitation

I was a husk,
    stumbling through days
    like a marionette of bone and sorrow.
    My heart silent,
    my skin gray,
    a creature half alive,
    numb with no rhythm.

But the world, patient,
    waited with its currents.
    Each laugh with a friend struck like a match.
    Every sunset stitched color back into my veins.
    Friends' voices carried sparks,
    small shocks that rattled me awake.

Day by day,
    the strings loosened
    and numbness drifted away.
    My limbs twitched,
    my chest lifted deeper.

Clear lightning found me,
    like paddles in an operating room
    setting fire to my pulse

shouting *clear!*
And restarted my zombie heart.

Now I am stitched in color,
    sewn in joy,
    alive with warmth and my own radiant thunder.
    This is no horror,
    this is resurrection.

I rose from my own grave,
    walk into the light,
    and burn brighter than ever before.

You Can Say It

For so long
   I didn't want to say it.
   Victim.
   Abused.
   Those words felt like I didn't deserve them.
   There are real victims out there.
   Those terms are reserved for those who endure.
   Physical violence. Flesh against flesh.
   He never raised a hand.
   He hit walls.
   He flipped couches.
   He stormed like thunder
   through every room.
   He implied.
   But he didn't hit me.
   And so I told myself
   it doesn't count.
   But the fear was real.
   The silence after his rage was real.
   Walking on eggshells was real.
   Shrinking of myself to avoid the storm was real.
   He didn't hit me.
   But he broke me.
   And I can finally say it.

He was an abuser.
And I was abused.

Then Why Did You Stay?

Because he wasn't always a monster.
  He was laughter and warmth,
    quiet evenings that felt like peace instead of pain.

Because he was my favorite person in the world.
  I thought I'd found *it,*
    my person, my happily ever after.

Because it came in patterns.
  Days, sometimes weeks of calm,
  until the air shifted,
  a word with teeth,
  a look that made me cry.
  Suddenly the eruption,
  rage scattering like marbles across the floor,
  pieces I picked up with trembling hands.

Because after the breaking,
  he became the balm.
  Flowers on the table,
  kisses like bandages.
  And I thought,
  maybe I made it worse in my head.
  Maybe I'm too sensitive.

Maybe I am just being dramatic.

Because he convinced me
   he was all I had.
   That leaving meant hunger,
   loneliness,
   a hollowed-out world
   without my best friend.

Because he was both the knife and the salve.
   The one who opened the wound
   and the one who kissed it closed.

Bacon

My mother lays bacon on a sheet,
    slides it into the oven.
    Simple. Peaceful.
    And I'm gone.
    I am back cooking BLTs for you.
    Heart pounding.
    Terrified of a sandwich.
    White bread. Lettuce. Tomato.
    A plate carried upstairs,
    to where you hide in your game.
    It was safest.
    The table was worse.
    Too many ways to fail.
    The memory stings.
    But on the scent of cooking grease, the memory over.
    And I'm back in my mother's kitchen,
    watching bacon crisp in peace.
    And it doesn't matter anymore.
    Because I'll never cook for you again.
    I will never be terrified of a sandwich again.
    Now I simply,
    eat the fucking bacon.

Never Ours

I had guessed you would give her
   a ring, a vow,
   something swift
   to anchor permanence.
   And I was right.
   Still, the news pressed heavy.
   Not envy.
   Not desire.
   Only the murmur
   of years I spent believing
   I would be the one
   to bear your future,
   to hold the life
   we once whispered about
   in the dark.
   But it isn't me.
   It's not us.
   The future was never ours.

Voyeur

You scroll through my life like a man at a keyhole,
    peering in from the dark.
    Do you like what you see?
    The light in my eyes, the ease in my smile,
    the woman you couldn't kill?
    Only I hold the key to let you back in,
    and I will never hand it out so freely again.
    Aren't you happy in your new life?
    Why do you stare into mine
    when your own flesh and blood
    crawls inside your home?
    Does it kill you to see me unbothered,
    thriving in your absence?
    Do you regret urging me to speak
    all the things I never said?

Forgive, Not Forget

Today I said it.
　I forgive you.
　Not because it was okay,
　not because I excuse it,
　but because I refuse to carry it anymore.
　I forgive you for me,
　for my peace,
　for the air I need to breathe.
　I don't hate you.
　I'm not angry.
　But I remember.
　I will always remember.

Sea Foam

I am sea foam.
  Born of rough waters,
  violence churning me into pieces,
  breaking me down until I dissolved.
  Washed ashore,
  what remains glistens under the sun.
  And when the wind moves me,
  I scatter,
  float away down the coast.
  Not destroyed.
  Not trapped.
  Free.
  I am sea foam.

Confetti

Memories fall like confetti in my mind.
  One moment I'm still,
  the next a fragment floats down.
  Childhood.
  My parents flipping the newspaper in bed.
  Heartbreak.
  The scent of his skin.
  A hallway.
  The smell of paint in my elementary school.
  Mrs. Robinson's class,
  an assignment to write one word that describes you,
  everyone else writing soccer, dance, football.
  I wrote *different*.
  I wanted to erase it.
  She wouldn't let me. I never forgot the lesson.
  That it's okay not to be the same.
  To lead instead of follow.
  I never know what confetti will appear next,
  which memory will float by.
  Some fragments glitter, some cut.
  All of them drift without cause, without reason.
  Confetti.
  Each piece drifts down,
  reminding me I am stitched

from fragments both beautiful and tragic,
a colorful rain,
its own kind of art.

Candy Cane Socks

Suddenly I am fourteen again,
　reminiscing on a first love
　that felt different than this.
　I am buzzing with the thrill of being seen.
　On a skating rink,
　he raced fast, effortless, free.
　He tied my skates for me.
　Holding my gloved hand,
　teaching me how to glide on ice.
　On the bus ride back
　we shared headphones,
　one in his ear,
　one in mine.
　His striped candy cane socks made me laugh.
　He fell asleep on my shoulder,
　and I felt like I'd stepped into a movie.
　It started with a wave in the hallway
　and from that moment came dances, proms,
　first one to hold my hand,
　first to wrap his arm around me,
　first kiss,
　first time.
　I was so young,
　not ready for forever.

But I carry him still,
the first love of my life.
Years have passed.
I hope he is happy.
And if he ever thinks of me,
I hope it is fondly.

The Day I Thought I Was Pretty

It started small.
I kept noticing my eyes.
Green with specks of brown,
bright like a place I hadn't been in years.
I stared, mesmerized.
Surely I'd have seen them before.
I look at myself every day.
But it was like seeing them for the first time.
Maybe part of me had died.
Maybe part of me had stood back up.
Either way,
something shifted.
I felt new.
I thought, *"you're kind of pretty."*
Once, I thanked him for loving me
even though I was ugly.
But he made me see myself that way,
didn't he?
But this day looking at my eyes,
I began to see myself again.

Traces

Barry Manilow on my screen
   and suddenly I'm back in time
   thinking again of my first love.
   How he loved musicals, hockey, and his family.
   Made me feel special.
   I remember his ambition, military dreams, candy cane socks.
   Conversations that lit me up.

I remember my second love.
   His fingers on a piano, songs in a cloud, lyrics written for me.
   Black framed glasses and blue eyes that saw me for me.
   His gentleness making me consider the meaning of life.

But this last love?
   I can't name a single thing about him.
   Not one.
   Because he wasn't real.
   He mimicked what he thought I wanted to see.
   He was thin air.
   There is only the list of what I endured under the spell.

I've forgiven myself.
   When you know better,
   you do better.

I see clearly now.
Real love leaves a trace.

I Am Who I Am

Look at me,
   I'm still here,
   still rising,
   still confident enough to walk into the world alone.
   Alone at the table,
   alone in the crowd,
   and I don't flinch.
   I don't apologize.
   This body carries me,
   this body survived,
   this body is mine.
   And I've decided I am who I am.
   Not hiding.
   Not shrinking.
   Not waiting for permission.
   I take up space.
   I belong.
   I am enough.
   And that is power.

Cotton Candy Sky

A cool breeze carried away your scent.
The warm ocean washed away our sins.
Waves stripped your hold from me
while the sand held me steady.
The Lord sat beside me,
His arm around my shoulder,
painting a cotton candy sky
with His other hand.
As I threw your trinkets
into the Atlantic,
I said goodbye forever.
I wondered where they'd drift,
might they float to the Titanic?
Far fetched, but I liked the thought.
Maybe someone will find the tangle,
wonder what happened,
read my story
and return them to the sea.

You Never Left

I asked where You were
   when I stayed too long,
   when my voice was silenced,
   when I rocked myself in the dark.
   And You said,
   "I was there
   in the whisper telling you to leave,
   in the strength helping you pack,
   in the breath when you thought you had run out of air."
   I thought I was abandoned.
   But I see it now,
   You never left.
   You carried me out.

Comeback

Today I danced around my kitchen.
Bare feet.
Bliss.
No stress.
No anxiety.
No him.
Just me,
so fucking light,
so fucking free.
Today I laughed.
I *laughed*.
A few months ago,
I couldn't imagine it.
But now,
I'm making a comeback.

To the Girl Who Rocked Herself

Sweetheart,
   I see you there,
   arms wrapped tight around yourself,
   while your world collapsed.
   You saved me.
   And you were right.
   It was okay.
   Because you lived.
   Now it's my turn.
   I'll hold you,
   I'll thank you,
   I'll never abandon you again.
   You carried me here,
   and here is beautiful.

Hopeful Thunder

I spend the day cleaning,
    casting out the relics of a haunted life.
    Anything that reminds me of you is gone.
    The couch where we sat,
    photos of us,
    cups that touched your lips.
    I'll call it what it is,
    an opportunity to cleanse my life of you.
    Lately,
    you're only a whisper.
    Not the crack of lightning and thunder you once were.
    Still, it's sad,
    to go from talking every day for years to nothing.
    I'd be lying if I said I didn't hope,
    I'm still a whisper to you too.
    Hell, I wouldn't mind
    being your thunder.

Holy Ground

The first time I felt God,
   as real as tide against skin was by the beach.
   I sat in the cooling sand,
   turning tokens of a lost love in my hand,
   ready to let them go and sink into the Atlantic's depths.
   He was there.
   White robes and hair in the breeze,
   bare feet in the sand next to mine.
   His arm around me,
   and I could *feel* Him.
   We shared no words, only silence.
   Like He wanted to be with me for this moment of goodbye.
   Peace like I had never known seeped into my veins,
   as I tossed tokens into the sea.
   The beach became holy ground.

P.S.

I talked to a boy last night.
    I was so nervous
    like a high school girl,
    moths fluttering in my stomach.
    Out of practice.
    Afterwards, I cried.
    Not because I missed you.
    I didn't.
    Not because I wanted you.
    I don't.
    You were just there.
    A shadow watching my conversation.
    Lingering at the edge of my something new.
    P.S. I Don't Still Love You.
    I don't even like you. Not anymore.
    And I love that for myself.

My Boy

You'll never know
   what you meant to me.
   We never met,
   yet you were a lifeline.
   You didn't see how your kindness
   steadied me.
   How your stories cut through the heaviness.
   You reminded me
   I could laugh again.
   I still think of the little things,
   salt water taffy, three cup of coffee kind of days,
   Halloween horror nights and tattoos,
   the board games you loved.
   They made me believe life could be playful again.
   I wanted to be ready for you,
   but I wasn't.
   And when you moved on I wasn't angry. Not at all.
   I only missed the lightness you gave me.
   Right guy, wrong time.
   That's how I'll remember you.
   I hope you found someone ready,
   someone who laughs with you the way I once did through a screen.
   And if you never know,
   that's okay.

I know.

And I'm grateful for you, B.

Another Day

And one day,
    you'll eat a breakfast sandwich again.
    The bread will be too toasted,
    the egg a little lopsided,
    the cheese slipping out the side.
    And it will be perfect.
    Not because of what it is,
    but because of what it isn't.
    It won't taste like survival.
    It won't carry the weight of memory.
    It won't belong to him.
    It will just be breakfast.
    You'll take a bite,
    wipe the corner of your mouth,
    sip your coffee,
    and smile at nothing in particular.
    It will be any other day.
    And that will be everything.

III

Healing

Thoughts of My Own

One day,
   a thought came that wasn't his.
   It was small.
   Simple.
   Like *I want coffee.*
   But it was mine.
   Not corrected,
   not doubted,
   not spun into madness.
   Just mine.
   That's when I knew
   my mind was home.

Glass Angels

Last night I dreamt of glass angels,
   tiny, shining things
   lined up on a shelf.
   They glittered in the light,
   fragile and unbroken,
   a chorus of quiet grace.
   I woke smiling
   as if heaven had whispered
   you are free,
   you are whole,
   you are blessed.
   And for the first time,
   I believed it.

Risen From Ruin

I loved you through ash,
    but I am not the wreckage.
    I have risen through ruin,
    and at last,
    I blaze.

Coffee in Peace

Steam curls from the mug,
   a little ceremony
   in the quiet of morning.
   I stir in cream,
   take the first sip,
   and smile.
   Freedom doesn't always look like fireworks.
   Sometimes it looks like coffee,
   sipped in peace.

Lipstick

I twist the tube,
　color rising like a flame.
　Bright red, soft peach, muted orange,
　he never allowed any of it.
　But this is not for him, it is in spite of him.
　I steady my hand,
　paint my lips slowly,
　as if crowning myself.
　Every swipe
　a gentle reminder
　I am allowed to be bold,
　to be seen.
　I lean into the mirror
　and there she is
　smiling back,
　soft and certain,
　a woman who belongs to herself.

Lipstick Vol. 2

I swipe on red
    the kind that glows loud in daylight.
    And then I laugh.
    Because it's perfect.
    I pucker at my reflection,
    strike a pose no one sees but me.
    Every shade I try is a secret celebration.
    The mirror winks back,
    and for once I like the girl smiling at me.
    She's daring.
    She's radiant.
    She's me.

I Was Never Ugly

I was never ugly.
   But I believed I was,
   wrapped myself in heavy sweaters,
   hid my skin, my smile, my light
   shrinking to fit inside your shadow.
   I thought your love was a gift
   I had to earn,
   a mercy I had to worship.
   But when you left,
   the mirror changed.
   The world brightened.
   And suddenly so did I.
   Now I see freckles like stardust,
   eyes glimmering with flecks
   of green, hazel, brown
   a whole universe,
   right here in me.
   I wear dresses that dance,
   lipstick that sings,
   skin that breathes summer
   without apology.
   I was never ugly.
   I never needed you
   to love hideous parts of me.

I was radiant all along.
And I never needed you,
I only needed to step into my own sunlight
and love the brilliance
that was always mine.

Learn to Fly

I used to think love
  meant saying yes.
  Yes to the silence.
  Yes to the weight.
  Yes to keeping the peace.
  Yes, even when it split me in two.
  But healing taught me
  that no is holy.
  No is a door I am allowed to choose.
  Now I carry my own keys.
  I decide who enters,
  who stays,
  who leaves.
  I deserve love that respects *no*,
  that honors *no*,
  that doesn't bruise my *no*
  into silence.
  Boundaries are not walls.
  They are wings.
  And finally,
  I know how to fly.

Better Man

Driving home,
   windows down,
   the air cool and soft
   against my skin.
   "Better Man" drifts through the speakers,
   once my anthem,
   once my ache.
   I skip it today.
   I don't wish he were better.
   I'm glad he's exactly who he is, wherever he is.
   As long as its not next to me.
   I feel peace.
   I feel light.
   I feel the road ahead open,
   the music my own,
   freedom in every breath,
   possibility in every turn.

Moth

I felt like a moth,
in a sky of butterflies.
Drawn to every flicker,
mistaking false light for truth
and let it scorch my wings.
But decay taught me,
a cocoon is not a coffin,
it is a door.
I broke it wide,
and remembered,
moths exist because of metamorphosis.
Wings painted in dust and shadow,
veins glowing with moonlight.
I am not a failed butterfly.
I am a moth.
Resilient, radiant, born of darkness,
yet luminous in my own sky.

Answered Prayers

I prayed for him to change.
   Begged, bargained,
   waited years.
   No answer.
   So one day I prayed differently.
   I didn't pray *make him better,*
   but instead prayed *give me peace. I pray for peace.*
   And God answered.
   With thunder.
   With lightning.
   With a door I finally walked through.

Marcy

When you know better, you do better.

Forgiving Horizons

I forgive the girl
   who stayed too long,
   who loved too hard,
   who forgot herself.
   She was doing her best.
   And now the world opens wide,
   an endless horizon,
   hers to claim.

Miami Goodbye

On the beach in Miami,
   I think of you.
   Not missing,
   just feeling your absence.
   How *good* it feels.
   Laughter, midnight pizza,
   a life that never existed in your world.
   Now I'm free.
   Now I'm me.

Glitter Pen Plans

I no longer hide from the future.
  I make plans,
  circle dates in glitter pen,
  fall asleep dreaming of places not yet mine.
  The road ahead beckons me,
  and I don't walk toward it,
  I run for it.

Someday

I will love again.
　Not with fear,
　not with bending,
　not with begging.
　But with laughter that feels easy,
　silence that feels safe,
　a hand that feels steady.
　And even if someday
　never comes,
　I have already found
　the love I needed most.
　My own.

Lighthouse

When the fog lifted,
   the world returned in color.
   Friends stood like lighthouses,
   glowing at the edges of my dark.
   Family reached for me,
   beacons steady on the shore
   guiding me home.

The light was always there.
   But my sight was clouded,
   a glass smeared with grief.
   I mistook the view for absence,
   the distance for loss.
   The light was always there.

Life, dazzling and bright,
   spilled back into me.
   The thrill of mornings,
   the shimmer of evenings,
   laughter ringing clear as bells.
   I hadn't felt this alive
   since girlhood,
   since the days I dreamed
   under endless skies,

believing joy was possible.

I see the beam sweep wide,
  I follow it home,
  and I believe again.
  The light was always there.

ILY

I used to be thankful for crumbs,
    called them love and swallowed my hunger whole.
    But now?
    I love myself.
    I love the sound of my laughter,
    the sharpness of my wit.
    I love my scars when they shine like constellations,
    mapping how far I've traveled.
    I love my softness,
    the way I care,
    the way I keep trying even when it hurts.
    I love that I am mine,
    not anyone's to claim.
    I am the love I always needed.

Pinky Promise

I'm sorry your little girl wandered
   deep into a fog.
   But I've found her again.
   And I pinky promise
   to guard her better.
   You taught me love
   is gentle, respectful, steady, kind.
   I won't forget again.
   I'll dance.
   I'll laugh.
   I'll wait for a love
   that feels like yours.

To the Stars Who Listen

It started with a simple text.
"Do you like to read?"
A universe opened and I fell into pages,
like falling into waiting arms.
Characters carrying hope when I had none.
Stories of courts and wings,
proved a better life,
a deeper,
kinder love *could* exist.
Night after night I whispered to the sky,
"to the stars who listen."
And now I believe dreams are not just wished,
they are answered.

Not By Time Alone

They will tell you time heals everything.
  That if you just wait,
  the ache will fade,
  the edges will soften,
  the wound will close.
  But it wasn't time that saved me.
  It was the nights I searched for language
  to name what had no name.
  The afternoons I shook in my car,
  and still walked through the door to be seen.
  The mornings I swallowed small circles of hope,
  and called it a step, not a shame.
  It was research.
  Reflection.
  Work.
  Misery.
  Returning to the scene
  again and again
  until the scene lost its teeth.
  I won't lie to you.
  Healing felt like dying first.
  Like ripping up carpet,
  to find rot underneath.
  Like standing barefoot,

on shards of my own story.
But listen,
I am still here.
I paint my nails red just because I like it.
I make coffee,
and it is only coffee.
If you are here and hurting,
thinking wounds are forever,
I promise you, it will close.
It will take more than time.
It will take everything you have,
and some things you don't know you hold yet.
It will take honesty,
and tears,
and days you won't believe me.
But healing is possible.
Even for wounds like ours.
Keep going.
I've got you.

And So We Must Say Goodbye

You've walked with me through shadows and storms,
 through silence that screamed
 and truths that cut.
 You've held the weight of my words
 and carried them as your own.
 For that, I thank you.
 If my scars have spoken to yours,
 know this,
 we are proof that healing is not only possible,
 it is happening.
 Even now, even here.
 And so we must say goodbye.
 But not the kind that ends,
 the kind that releases.
 I leave you with this,
 your voice is worthy,
 your body is yours,
 your life is not finished.
 Carry these pages as a lantern,
 but do not mistake them
 for your light.
 That light was always yours.

Echoes at the End

I carried the noise for years,
   but echoes fade.
   Close the book,
   the echo of all the things I've finally said
   ends right here.

www.ingramcontent.com/pod-product-compliance
Lightning Source LLC
Chambersburg PA
CBHW020418150626
46554CB00014B/1934